T5-AFQ-068

Lance Laguna's

Dance! Dance! Dance!

Lance Laguna's

Dance! Dance! Dance!

Master Six Ballroom Dances

RUNNING PRESS
PHILADELPHIA · LONDON

Library of Congress Cataloging-in-Publication Number
00-131313

ISBN 0-7624-0826-X

This book may be ordered by mail from the publisher.
Please include $1.00 for postage and handling.
But try your bookstore first!

Running Press Book Publishers
125 South Twenty-second Street
Philadelphia, Pennsylvania 19103-4399

Visit us on the web!
www.runningpress.com

Contents

Pull up a chair—
and let's talk dancing!

After working on cruise
ships for more than twenty
years, I know I can teach
anyone how to dance.
Bashful newlyweds? No
problem. Arthritic senior
citizens? Piece of cake. On
a typical six-night cruise, my
students master six of the
world's most popular ball-

room and Latin dances: the
Waltz, Fox-Trot, Merengue,
Cha-Cha, Tango, and Swing.
    These classes are a
source of great pride to
me. I love watching my students blossom and flourish.
We often establish close,
personal relationships. And
when the end of the week
comes, saying goodbye is
always hard. There is lots
of crying and hugging.

Rio de Janeiro, 1979

Some women even beg
me to come with them—
to live in their little towns
of Cedar Rapids or Walla
Walla or Poughkeepsie.
But I must always respect-
fully decline. I have an
obligation, you see, to the
cruise ship passengers
of tomorrow.

 This book is a gift to
my students. Here are the
lessons that forged our

relationship. Here is a
miniature Lance Laguna
that you may carry wher-
ever you go. I hope you
will cherish these lessons
forever, just as I cherish
my memories of you.

Lance Laguna
Galápagos Islands,
Ecuador
June, 2000

The Rules of Dance

Once, on a cruise bound for Tierra del Fuego, I danced with a beautiful dental hygienist, Marion, who insisted that dancing had no rules. Later that night, she proved her point when we danced the Tango in her single wide-berth cabin. But on a public dance floor, I urge my students to follow these general guidelines.

For the Gentleman

• Always begin with your left foot—no exceptions.

• Don't play "Statue of Liberty" with your left arm. A left arm held too high is uncomfortable for your partner and unsightly on the dance floor.

• Don't tell the lady what you're trying to do—talking will only spoil your

mystique. The ideal gentleman leads with confidence and sheer animal magnetism.

• Don't hold your lady too tightly. A dancing woman is like a kite—turning, falling, and soaring through the air. You can *direct* her, but must not control her.

• Don't pump your arms in time to the music.

16

This is only acceptable
in novelty routines such
as The Chicken Dance.
• Never participate in
novelty routines such
as The Chicken Dance.

For the Lady

• Always begin with your
right foot (usually step-
ping backwards). Step
onto the sole first, then

let the heel fall gracefully
and naturally.

• Don't lean or hang on ➤
your partner like a dead
mink. This can suggest a
feeling of "baggage" that
many gentlemen find
uncomfortable. Stay light
on your feet!

• Be patient with the gentleman, and don't try to
anticipate his moves. If
you're frustrated by his

Dance! Dance! Dance!

lack of skill, it is better to switch partners then to subvert his authority.

◄ • Lean back slightly into the gentleman's right arm; this will allow him to lead you more easily, and suggests a measure of trust that can be very attractive.

• Don't clench his hand too tightly. Remember: You're dancing, not thumb-wrestling!

Choosing a Partner

*Y*our partner is crucial to your success. When scouting the dance floor for potential candidates, be sure to avoid the following:

Drill Sergeants can ruin a perfectly good Cha-Cha with their relentless chanting of "left, right, left right left."

Floor hogs insist on demonstrating their fantastic skills to all of the other dancers—while taking up the space of four or five couples. If you've got Lance Laguna moves, share them with your partner, not the entire ballroom!

Empowered women refuse to be led. Although

I wholeheartedly support
equality for women in the
workplace, I must insist
the gentleman retains control on the dance floor.
The alternative is chaos
and confusion on a scale
we cannot imagine.

Songbirds serenade their
partners by humming
unintelligibly into their
ears. Some will even

whisper the lyrics of
"Beautiful Dreamer"
or "Oye Como Va."

Statues can be recognized
a mile off by their glassy-
eyed stare, pursed lips,
and stiff movements. They
can make the steamiest
Tango seem duller than
the Hokey Pokey.

Self-proclaimed instructors will stop in the middle of the dance to teach their partners a new move, whether their partners want to learn it or not. Trust me: Unless your partner is a licensed and certified N.S.O.D.A. Instructor of Dance (like myself), you can skip their lessons.

Perfect partners are courteous, considerate, and respectful of dance floor etiquette. A gentleman will lead confidently but not too forcefully; a lady will be graceful and accommodating. Patience and a good sense of humor are also important— remember, you're supposed to be having fun!

Posture

One of the most rewarding benefits of dance is improved posture. Remember: You dance not only with your feet, but also with your arms, your torso, your neck, and your head. To dance comfortably and accurately, good posture must be maintained at all times. Keep these suggestions in mind as you practice:

Dance! Dance! Dance!

- Stand up straight, but not stiff, and hold your head high.
- Look forward (not down to your feet).
- Keep your chest out and your shoulders back— stand tall but also limber and relaxed.
- Bend your legs ever so slightly. Never lock your knees!

The Frame

*T*he Frame is the manner in which the gentleman holds the lady.

It is also known as *closed position*, and varies slightly in the Latin dances and Swing.

1. Dancers stand tall with feet close together.
2. Arms are raised, with elbows away from the body.

3. Gentleman places his right hand on the lady's back—just below her left shoulder blade.

4. He holds her parallel to him, and slightly to his right.

5. Gentleman holds left hand up, about eye level, elbow away from body and slightly bent.

6. Lady places right hand in gentleman's left,

between his forefinger
and thumb.

7. She rests her left arm
lightly on his right arm
and the rest of her hand
on his shoulder.

8. Dancers should main-
tain a slight but comfort-
able resistance.

9. The gentleman looks
over the lady's right shoulder; she looks over his
right shoulder.

Laguna Lingo

*h*ere are some basic terms I'll be using to teach the lessons in this book.

Rhythm cues: These specify the rhythm of the music, and it helps to concentrate on these cues while you practice (when Swing dancing, for example, you'll keep a Slow Slow Quick Quick count in your head).

41

Remember: Slow= 2 beats
and Quick= 1 beat.

Style: These notes indicate
the spirit and flavor of the
dance, from the graceful
waltz to the steamy tango.

Smooth Moves: These are
variations that will take
you beyond the basic step.
Some are tricky—but if
you do them well, you'll be
the most popular person
on the dance floor!

Lesson One: The Waltz

*i*n the early 17th century—long before Dirty Dancing and the Lambada—waltzing was considered vulgar because of its close holds and quick turns. Derived from the old German word *walzen*—meaning to glide, roll, or turn—the Waltz originated as a peasant dance in Vienna, but was embraced by high society during the

45

18th century. These days, it remains a popular favorite, and is a great place to start dancing.

Style: Waltzing is characterized by a graceful wave-like motion of the body. You'll need to stay extra loose on this one. Dancers should bend their knees on the first step, then rise smoothly on the second and third steps (called balance steps).

Rhythm Cues: Quick, Quick, Quick.
Listen to the music and you'll hear a steady "1,2,3" rhythm.

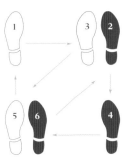

**gentleman
start here**

Gentleman: Forward, Balance,

Balance; Back, Balance, Balance.

All steps are Quick steps.

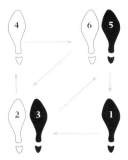

lady start here

Lady: Back, Balance, Balance;

Forward, Balance, Balance.

All steps are Quick steps.

Smooth Moves:

Lady's Turns: **No Waltz** is complete without one good lady's turn. While stepping backwards with his right foot, the gentleman should signal a turn by raising his left arm over his partner's head (he may also guide her to turn with his right hand). The lady steps toward him with

her left foot, pivots to her right, and then steps on her left, all while turning in a clockwise direction under his arm. (He should continue doing his basic step throughout the entire turn.) The couple may then resume closed position.

Quarter Turns: Without these, you'll be stuck in a

simple box step all night—
and where's the fun in
that? Quarter Turns allow
you to circle around the
dance floor, and they're
incredibly simple: Both
dancers should step 90
degrees to their left every
time they move forward
or backward. After four
basics—or twelve steps
total—you'll return to
where you began.

Lesson Two: The Fox Trot

five years ago, on an excursion to the Tonga Islands, I gave private lessons to a famous Hollywood actress—I won't reveal her name, but let's just say she had a "basic instinct" for dance! She also claimed to be a descendent of vaudeville performer Harry Fox, who dazzled audiences in the 1920s with his unusual

55

mix of slow and quick dance steps. Spectators described the phenomenon as "Fox's Trot," and the rest is history.

Style: The modern Fox Trot is smooth and flowing; feet should be close to the floor. You'll need to master two steps: the Magic Step and the West Chester. Switching from

one form to the other
requires a graceful touch
and excellent leading ability.

Magic Step (Traveling)
Rhythm Cues:
Slow, Slow, Quick Quick.

West Chester (Basic Box)
Rhythm Cues:
Slow, Quick Quick.

Magic Step (Traveling)

quick

3 4 2

quick

slow

Gentleman:
Forward, Forward,
Side together

1

slow

slow

**gentleman
start here**

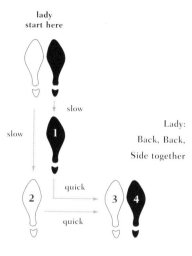

lady start here

slow

1

slow

2

quick

3 **4**

quick

Lady:
Back, Back,
Side together

West Chester (Basic Step)

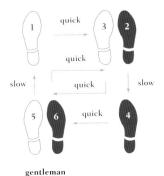

**gentleman
start here**

Gentleman: Forward (slow), Right (quick) together (quick); Back (slow), Left (quick) together (quick)

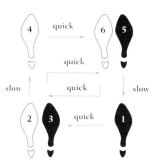

Lady: Back (slow), Left (quick)
together (quick); Forward (slow),
Right (quick) together (quick)

Smooth Moves

Lady's Turn: Just like a turn in the Waltz. While stepping backwards with his right foot, the gentleman should signal a turn by raising his left arm above his partner's head (he may also guide her to turn with his right hand). The lady steps toward him with her left foot, pivots to her

right, and turns clockwise
underneath his arm.
(The gentleman should
continue doing the Basic
Box throughout the entire
turn.) The couple may
then resume closed
position.

Quarter Turns: As with the
Waltz, Quarter Turns in
the Fox Trot allow you to
circle around the dance

floor. Both dancers should step 90 degrees to their left every time they step forward or backward. You should complete a full 360-degree turn in twelve steps.

Promenade: While executing the Magic Step, both partners should turn forty-five degrees, so they are facing (and walking) in the same direction. The

gentleman turns left; the lady turns right.

Gentleman: The gentleman steps forward with two slow steps—first left, then right—and turns back into closed position. He finishes with two quick steps—first left, then right. I sometimes use this opportunity to give my partner a quick kiss on the cheek, but use your own

discretion before adding
this smooth move.
Lady: The lady steps
forward with two slow
steps—first right, then
left—and turns back into
closed position. She finishes with two quick steps—
first right, then left. If the
lady is feeling frisky, she
may also use this opportunity to steal a kiss.

Lesson Three: The Merengue

*i*n the late 1980s, on a cruise bound for Sri Lanka, I spent a week with a lovely marine biologist, Guadalupe, who told me the Merengue was the national dance of her native Dominican Republic. Although the origins of the dance are unclear, Lupe believed it began in the plantation fields, where chained slaves were forced to drag one leg as they harvested sugar. A few months ago, I saw my precious Lupe on a PBS documentary; she commented on the "underwater dance" of marine life, and I knew I was still in her heart.

Style: Elbows should be bent and almost touching—but otherwise, it's all

in the hips! Drop your hip as you take the first step, then shift your weight with the second step. If the mood is right, gaze passionately into your partner's eyes.

Rhythm Cues: Step, Drag. It doesn't get any easier than this. The Merengue consists of a step followed by a drag step.

gentleman
start here

step

drag

step

drag

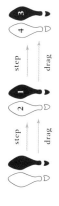

step

drag

step

drag

lady
start here

Smooth Moves:

Lady's Turn: The gentleman should signal a turn by raising his left arm just above his partner's head (he may also guide her to turn with his right hand). She releases her left hand as she turns under his arm in eight steps—all while keeping the rhythm in her hips. The gentleman

does his basic in place
before they resume closed
position. The lady may
turn back the same way
she came.

The Cuddle: The gentleman raises his left arm, allows the lady to walk underneath it, and drops the arm so that she is wrapped up in a "cuddle." This should take four Merengue steps. The couple may dance in place, or the gentleman may reverse these moves to return the lady to the conversation position.

The Flirt: A fun move if you know your partner (and even more fun if you don't!) the flirt lets you move from conversation to closed position. The gentleman simply raises the lady's left hand, drapes it behind his head, and lets her arm fall to his shoulder, ending in closed position.

Lesson Four: The Tango

*W*omen always plead with me to dance the tango—and yet very few realize this dance originated in turn-of-the-century Argentina, as a ritual between prostitutes and their pimps! Later, it was imported to Paris, refined by French high society, and stripped of its negative connotations. Today, the tango may seem

exaggerated and theatrical—
but a red-hot passion still
smolders beneath its surface.

Style: The tango character-
istically features stalking,
predatory gliding steps and
a sense of flirtatious com-
bat between partners.

Rhythm Cues: Slow, Slow,
Quick Quick, Slow.

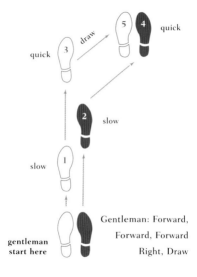

draw

quick

5

4

quick

slow

2

slow

quick

3

1

gentleman
start here

Gentleman: Forward,
Forward, Forward
Right, Draw

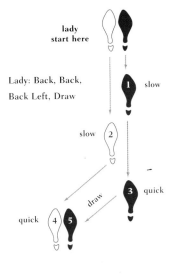

**lady
start here**

Lady: Back, Back,
Back Left, Draw

1 slow

2 slow

3 quick

draw

4 quick

5

Smooth Moves

Promenade: The gentle-
man begins by turning
the lady into promenade
position. He steps left
(slow), then right (slow),
and then makes a quarter
turn to the left (quick).
He closes with the last
two steps of the tango
basic (quick slow).

Dance! Dance! Dance!

The lady steps right (slow),
then left (slow), where she
pivots counter-clockwise
in a quarter turn before
finishing with the end
of the tango basic (quick
quick slow). Whenever I
dance the Tango, I like
to "whip" the lady around
as I make my quarter
turn–this adds a nice
touch of style.

Corte: To lead, the gentleman pulls strongly towards himself on the back of the lady as he moves into Corte position. The gentleman lunges back on his left foot while the lady lunges forward with her right. This position is held on the slow slow beats. They then pick up the end of the tango basic with quick quick slow.

Leg Crawl: One of the sexiest ways to finish the Tango Corte is with a leg crawl. To accomplish this eye-catching move, the lady slides her left knee up the gentleman's right leg, ending with a pointed toe just above his shin. The shorter the skirt, the more dramatic the effect. (But not *too* short, ladies, please!)

Lesson Five: The Cha Cha

One night in the mid-1970s, I gave lessons to a shy but beautiful Cuban girl who would later become an international pop star. As we danced, she told me that the Cha-Cha began in her native country as a modified version of the Rhumba. Many years later, I saw one of her music videos on VH-1, and real-

97

ized she was still using
my teachings! (And Gloria,
if you're reading this,
*siempre tendras un lugar
en mi corazon!*)

Style: Couples may
dance in the traditional
closed position or in the
Challenge position, where
the gentleman drops the
lady's hands and they
dance individually. The

heart of this dance—the "cha cha cha"—is three small, syncopated steps. This "triple step" should be danced lightly, while the other steps should be accentuated and placed on the ball of the foot.

Rhythm Cues: step, step, cha cha cha.

step
step

cha
cha
cha

cha
cha
cha

cha
cha
cha

lady
start here

step
step

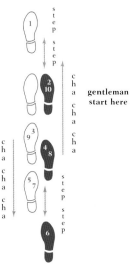

step step

cha cha cha

gentleman
start here

cha cha cha

step step

Smooth Moves

Lady's Turn
Gentleman: After his first triple step, the gentleman raises his left arm (signaling he intends to turn his partner) and guides the lady through the turn with his right hand, all while continuing his basic step. The lady will move forward left, pivot onto her

103

right, and take her cha-
cha steps while turning
right, until she is back
in the closed position.

Chase Turns: When executed
correctly, it will look like
the couple is playfully
chasing each other. The
lady and gentleman each
have a distinct set of
steps to follow.

Gentleman: The gentleman drops the lady's hands, signaling a move into challenge position. He steps forward with his left, pivots clockwise onto his right, then completes his cha-cha steps in the opposite direction. He steps forward with his right, then pivots to his left counter-clockwise, then takes his cha-

cha steps in the original
direction.

Lady: The gentleman will
turn away from the lady
as she takes her back step
(indicating he wants to do
a chase turn). She continues her basic until the
step forward. She steps
forward left, pivots clockwise onto her right, then
takes her cha-cha steps
in the opposite direction.

Then she steps forward right, pivots counter-clockwise left, and takes her cha-cha steps in the original direction. The most important move, of course, is to look like you're having fun!

Lesson Six: Swing

history: Also termed the Lindy, the Lindy Hop, and the Jitterbug, Swing began in the jazz-loving black communities of the early 1920s, and soon took America by storm. Thanks to a major resurgence in the late 1990s, you can now find supper clubs and swing ballrooms in cities across the United States. These

Gentleman: Left (slow), Right (slow), Back (quick) Left (quick rock step).

Lady: Right (slow), Left (slow), Back (quick) Right (quick rock step).

establishments are the
perfect chance to practice
your skills between cruises.

Style: Compared to other
more traditional ballroom
dances, the swing frame
is loose and relaxed.
Never lock your knees.

Rhythm Cues: Slow, Slow,
Quick Quick.

Smooth Moves

Lady's Turn: The gentleman raises his left arm, signaling a turn. The lady steps right under the man's arm, completes the turn with her left foot, then rock-steps with her right foot. Meanwhile, the gentleman continues with the basic step. From here, they may resume the basic,

or the lady may turn back
the way she came.

Conversation Position:
Some swingin' couples
prefer to dance in the
conversation position—
the gentleman holds the
lady's right hand with
his left, and holds her
left hand with his right.

Cuddle: Beginning in the conversation position, the gentleman raises his left arm to his right. The lady walks underneath his arm and allows herself to be wrapped up in his arms, while the man continues with his basic step. The couple then does the back step together, side by side. They may exit this position by going back the same way.

117

120

121

Discography

Many students think they
need to buy a bunch of
new albums to practice
dance—but that's not the
case. Ballroom dancing
has become so influential,
many of us don't even rec-
ognize a Waltz when we
hear one! A quick glance
through your record col-

lection will probably reveal dozens of Cha-Chas, Fox Trots, and much more. So fire up your turntable and get ready to get down!

Waltz

Enya: "Carribbean Blue"

Simply Red: "If You Don't Know Me by Now"

Cat Stevens: "Morning Has Broken"

Henry Mancini: "Moon River"

Van Morrison: "Straight to Your Heart (Like a Cannonball)"

Fox Trot
Harry Connick, Jr.: "It Had to be You"
Frank Sinatra: "Love and Marriage"
Van Morrison: "Moondance"
Natalie Cole: "Unforgettable"

Merengue
Ricky Martin: "Livin La Vida Loca"
Buster Poindexter: "Hot, Hot, Hot"
Paul Simon: "Late in the Evening"

Tango
ABBA: "Money, Money, Money"
Elton John: "Part Time Lover"
Strictly Ballroom Soundtrack

Cha-Cha

Madonna: "Papa Don't Preach"
Santana: "Oye Como Va"
Looking Glass: "Brandy"
Julio Iglesias: "Moonlight Lady"

Swing

Jim Croce: "Bad, Bad Leroy Brown"
Elvis Presley: "All Shook Up"
Wham!: "Wake Me Up
Before You Go-Go"
The Stray Cats: "Rock This Town"

Running Press would like to
extend a special thank-you
to The Five Spot in
Philadelphia, Pennsylvania,
and to our five fabulous models:

Toni Leslie
Katherine Wohlsen
Victor Golkow
Ann Golkow
Danielle McCole

You can e-mail Lance Laguna at:
laguna@victordance.com

This book has been bound
using handcraft methods
and Smyth-sewn to
ensure durability.

The dust jacket and interior were
photographed by Steve Belkowitz
and designed by Terry Peterson.

The text was written by
Jason Rekulak and Emily Grosvenor.

Expert dance guidance and
consultation provided by
Victor Golkow and Ann Golkow.

Dance shoes provided by
www.annsdanceboutique.com

The text was set in
Fairfield and Spring.